JN440342

A Boy Is Looking at the White Moon from a Classroom Under the Sea

(In memory of the late poet Seoung Chan-gyeong)

A Boy Is Looking at the White Moon from a Classroom Under the Sea

A collection of new poems by Jang I-ji
Translated by Jeon Seung-hee

Contents

A BOY IS LOOKING AT THE WHITE MOON FROM A CLASSROOM UNDER THE SEA

K POET

Midday

There are people living in villages both before and behind!

How wonderful it is to be able to see other people!

It's great to stand in the field in midday, the time belonging almost solely to the sky

And not to cry, but to watch dandelion spores flying and fluttering.

At last, I could talk to those people.

I can talk with them about that weightless clouds' way.

Rosy Cheeks, White Hair

Outside of the world
On a snow-covered mountaintop
A flower blooms under the moonlight
Once every 20 to 30 years.

And

Beyond that flower,

They say is a place to which the love we have lost has gone.

That it's a place which is impossible—truly impossible.

When in winter, the time when you left,

That flower blooms

For the first time after 20 or 30 years,

If a red flower blooms,

Days, hovering around it,

I will say that I'd like to offer what I don't have,

That I want to give you what I don't have,

Days, when I'll wax older, beating my chest.

Waterfall

—Senju Hiroshi*

While needleleaf trees become dark, broadleaf trees are transformed into deer. The forest is a dark stream. As the stars pour down over the valley, distinctions disappear. The sky is now the earth, colored with colorless water. The deer quietly listen to the sound of the stream. Down, down, further down—the water seems to say. Like fallen Adam and Eve, the waterfall pours to its lowest point. If nobody listens to that sound, it's as if the waterfall does not exist. The black gypsum where the entire universe sank down. A streak of descent that breaks

* Senju Hiroshi (1958-) is a Japanese Nihonga painter known for his large-scale waterfall paintings. [All footnotes in this book are added by the translator.]

it. A sinister white. At its bottom, the waterfall creases, again becoming flat. I drink. I try dipping my feet. The water creases and becomes placid.

Early Summer

The summer lilyturfs
Are giving approximately one-tenth of their green
To the wind.

Fattened with pollen, Itajii clouds,
Which have floated up in yellow,
Give about three-tenths of their pollen
To the wind.

Somehow, under the Itajii trees
You see a lot of dried leaves on the ground.
Under the Itajii trees
You hear the brown sound of the leaves crumbling.

Therefore I imagine something like

A transparent burlap bag, hanging on the back of the wind,

And wonder what in me flows into the world

To make the world glitter with such a sad color.

Hibiscus

A round sky pools in the stone mortar filled with water,
And on the spot where the sun is,
A white hibiscus flower overlaps with it.

The back of a person.
Her beautiful hairpin
Is floating up.
Inside the water mirror, the flower is virtuous.

Her voice is floating up.
Her face is not.
She is looking back at me.

The white flower is covering her face.

To let the sun float on the water,
The sky goes down under the water.
The most tranquil sun is
The hibiscus floating on the water.

On the water
I build a house out of a white shadow.
I build the house I left.

Postcard
—to a girl

Acorns that you left with me last year
Have become a song instead of acorn trees.
When I hold them in my palms,
The winds run toward me and tell the story of a faraway place,

That you have become an old woman, with sunken eyes,
And are alone in the dark,
Where there is neither the sky nor the earth.
It's not true, is it? It's a lie, right?

In the August sky, the blue floats.

A red dragonfly hovers,
Gathering the silver rays of the summer sun.
The trees have no problems.
They grow new moss under their shade.

In the universe of acorns you left with me,
The moon is hardening into a diamond,
And the stars are becoming calm and retired, like opal, to eventually become opal.
Birds at night become rocks on the field and fall asleep,
And wake up again as sparrows in the morning and flock around.

I'll wait for you.

It's okay if you've become an old woman,

In the midst of this festival of beings.

Searching for the Sky

—shape shift

They say the color of the sky reflects the color of the sea.

But in fact the color of the sky is a copy of the inside of the pink butterfly shell.

The child thinks the real sky is inside the butterfly shell.

Forgetting that it's dinner time,

He rummages through a mound of shells, squatting.

He is looking for the sky, until his mother comes looking for him.

How many colors of the sky brim over the waves!

After the mother and son return home,

The sky shines inside a pink butterfly shell behind them.

Blue Ink

—Roland Barthes

After Roland had died,

In his room,

They found 13,000 index cards.

Out of the lot, 320

Were titled "Mourning Diary."

Although some corrections were made in a black ballpoint pen or pencil,

Most were written in blue ink.

This bundle of cards is kept in a library in Europe,

And is rarely open to the public.

It makes me wonder

Whether the blue ink fades, or remains the same,

Whether it has not yielded to time,
Whether one's sadness does not in fact decrease
after the bomb of one's crying.

Whether, like disciples who would never budge
In the face of the earth guards' firepower,
Sadness can neither collapse nor be overthrown.

Sea Monster

Faraway, there is a beach below.

Something black is crossing the sea.

Occasionally, it reveals its dorsal fin.

And the sea swells in green and indigo.

Water scales are shining even more brightly than the sky.

The skin of the sea is blazing up white.

It does not land, just staring at my direction.

My skin is being pared in the salty sea wind.

Coral breaks to become white sands.

I wonder what broke to become clouds.

And basalt breaks to become black sands.

A monster that has been crossing the sea does not land, just looking at my direction.

Standing as a black cliff, it wraps around and raises up the waves.

Pricked by blue glass fragments, it also bleeds.

It's so sorrowful—I wonder what broke to become that altar of stacked clouds.

I stand as a platinum flame.

I become a blazing wind.

A Walk

Gardenias send white waves toward the sky.
They draw the sky toward themselves.
The sky lowers considerably
And sends blue waves over the flowers.
That is, it draws the gardenias toward itself.

Standing beside the gardenias, I tried to pull the sky,
In vain.
There is no gap in the gravitation pull between the flowers and sky.
They are neck and neck—there is no place for me between them.

Going down, as the black shadow of a black cat,
I quietly wait.
Until next year's lilies of the valley make the wind chime ring,
I will not make friends.
I will just continue to write poems.

Poems that will evaporate when touched by the light,
Poems I won't be disappointed about, even if they evaporate.

Scotland

Father digs up peat and I pick it up and gather it.

Elder sister breaks violet heather and makes a bouquet,

And the flames become red hot inside Mother's wood-burning stove.

In the high-dimensional time and space, dyed in heather color,

A layer of a thin evening opens up,

And miniature bulbs in the sky brighten the lights of their own small narratives.

It is then that the family gathers around the dinner table.

The smoke from the peat rises endlessly and accumulates again in the strata of time.

An Ark

Over the struggle of the sea, a ship is moving. A woman who died in April looks at the clouds.* *Going to Japan now?* A man who died in April fumbles around the horizon, blazing in blackening red.

A ship is floating ahead. A boy is looking at the white moon from an undersea classroom.** *How many more nights will it take to get to Jeju?* A humpback whale follows the stern of the ship, with a gigantic cry.

* April refers to the Jeju Uprising, also known as the Jeju April 3 Incident (April 1948-May 1949). Residents of Jeju Island protested peacefully against the division of Korea, but were brutally massacred by the military.

** This stanza refers to the 2016 Sinking of Sewol Ferry Incident, in which 304 passengers and crew died, including some 250 students from a high school in Ansan, a city near Seoul, on their way to Jeju Island from Incheon.

People who died in May and were buried in the May sky climb onto the deck in threes and fives.[***]

A child from Ansan nods. He's wearing clothes like a star and glitters in yellow.

When mountain folk, killed by the punitive expedition, ask when the uprising is going to be over, someone answers, *April never ends*, while pointing to the transparent musical score of a whirlpool.

The saint of Tharsis who fixes ships

Busily comes and goes over the sea of jelly.

[***] May refers to the 1980 Gwangju Uprising, in which citizens of Gwangju protested the new military junta and were massacred.

Under the waterline, it's all April.

*All of them are May, Yeosu, and Suncheon.*****

They are in pain. In pain.

Boys who look like high school students are taking water-green selfies against the backdrop of the forest of Seongpanak Peak. Trees rise toward the mirror on the mountaintop. Broken ships meet one another in front of the door of the mirror.

An ark is floating ahead deep into the sky.

**** May, Yeosu, and Suncheon refer to the Jeju Uprising and the 1948 Yeosu-Suncheon Rebellion, an incident of military rebellion protesting the government's brutal suppression of the Jeju Uprising.

On an Autumn Night
—Sowol*

The square sky melts into water, white and long.

The sun's concentric circles are reddening and scattered into clouds harboring rain.

The autumn mountain, bleeding in dark red, flows down,

Down to the outside of the village entrance.

The wind pushes me painfully toward the water village.

On my every empty step, after being pushed, the smell of soil darkens.

* Sowol primarily refers to Kim Sowol (1902-34), a poet famous for his contributions to early modern poetry. Throughout his life he wrote poignant poems in a style reminiscent of traditional Korean folk songs.

When stars sprout in this water village,

And the fish painstakingly swim around in the cold sky,

Where is she? If she is around, she must be in this enormous fusion.

Embracing an overturned sky, the water becomes heavier.

Water that does not reflect is asleep.

Amidst the tiny stars, the sound of laughter from bygone days

Swells up and dies down

Deep into the sky

On this autumn night.

Then All The Light
—Jeju, April 3

When a bee falls asleep atop a flower, the flower also recedes into its nectar, closes its eyes, and takes a rest.

On top of a rape blossom, a bee is sleeping—unaware of who is coming from inside the pistils.

Survivors deserted their homes and went to a mountain. They lived inside caves, subsisting on ferns. They lived while gnawing at darkness. Human boars were scurrying around on the mountain and digging up the earth. Eating ferns in the pitch darkness, people became dispirited. They were worried about their deserted houses. They were worried about their dead homes.

People with good ears could see the inside of a rock. When a person came out of a rock, those with good ears saw him, and, gradually, others could see him, too. People fumbled along a road of snakes and centipedes—that rough road of coagulated time—eating tiny pebbles and darkness. Throwing away broken vessels, throwing away soiled shoes, too, they reached the wormhole of deep roots.

When pistils opened up, they were all cuts and bruises—

Then all the light.

Between Earth's Horizon and Sea's Horizon

The sea horizon floats above the earth horizon.

On the other side of them, you
Are making clouds by shaking a pillow filled with feathers,

Painting the evening on the sky
By dipping the tail of the wind-dog into paint,

And writing a diary
While listening to the radio of moonlight.

As the space between the sea horizon and earth

horizon is my mind, which cannot be expressed in words,

A few things as bright and lonely as fishing lights are glittering there,

And the rest
Is all the blind sea undulating,
While the sound of waves rises and subsides in black—

Only that sea, the eyes which are spoiled by the sea horizon.

Chinkle-Chankle

"You won't gallop any more, Alan."
—from *Equus*, by Peter Shaffer

Someday you probably will not have pain any more. You probably will be released from the **chinkle-chankle** and will stride energetically on the street. You will probably work in a company with a lot of stairs. You will probably become a father. You will probably do stocks and gain and lose some money. You will probably forget everything. You will probably forget that you have run around the sky as a horse, holding **chinkle-chankle** in your mouth. You will probably forget that a flower of secret bloomed from the saliva flowing down in between **chinkle-chankle**; that various signs of nondaily life sprouted there. You will probably conk out after swimming or playing soccer with children once in a long while. While having mild fever, you might consider it strange that you don't have pain any more. You might consider it fortunate. You'll get your audience. You'll talk to your audience—with your mouth, from which **chinkle-chankle** has disappeared. Overjoyed with happiness, you might occasionally worry about me. You will probably end up not galloping. You will probably have pain no longer.

Apple of Tomorrow
—Miyazawa Kenji*

If I enter the depression in an apple, I find myself in the hidden evening of tomorrow. In the past, when Grandfather cut the heart of that earth in half, a few small hidden doors fell down. When I become curious about tomorrow, I do the gymnastics of watching an apple. I move my gaze from one spot to another about an inch apart. Following the surface of an apple, I approach its depression. But I don't bite. I don't make a pretty bite mark in order to prevent tomorrow from leaking out. Unlike Eve, unlike Snow White, I do gymnastics of watching an

* Miyazawa Kenji (1896-1933) was a Japanese novelist and poet of children's literature as well as an agricultural science teacher, a vegetrarian, cellist, devout Buddhist, and utopian social activist.

apple. When I enter the depression of an apple, I can see myself cross the atmosphere, hanging onto the apple blossoms. Inside the flesh of an apple it is entirely music covered with clouds. It's the tomorrow I long for.

Water Mother

I go to the aquarium on a rainy day. Looking at a jellyfish, I feel calmer. Flawless seniority of the Cambrian period five billion years ago. The skirt of the moon illuminating the bottom of the sea, without ever setting, for five billion years. Even without a brain, it is already a gesture. Even without a brain, it open the transparent door to the abyss. With an undecipherable gesture, outside of language, in a place where the light of language does not reach, it blazes.

I heard that it has a nickname: "Water Mother." A long skirt, fluttering. A boy holds onto the skirt of his mother and shakes it. The mother holds his hand tightly.

The Clouds Are So Thick That You Don't Know Where You Are*

A flower is already a part. Even before shedding its petals,
It is a part.
As what is left in the world is a flower,
I shed tears over the petals, and fill
Its shade with things like the sound of insects crying.
As I cannot fill this shade,
I anxiously hover around the flower.
Dropping kisses and embraces,
I try to fill the hole, and write a letter
On the petals. *How are you?* A flower is

* This title is a phrase from a poem, "Xunyinzibuyu," by Jia Dao (779-843), a Tang dynasty poet.

A wall with thorns. I write a letter

On the petals. *How are you doing?* (The letter always

Changes into a knot, a scar in gothic).

I plead with the flower, or the wall.

At that moment, a boy

Appears from nowhere, and this boy under a pine tree

Silently points to—a place where there are thick clouds,

An unknowable place. Between the clouds and me,

There is **a wall with thorns.**

Song of a Side*

On the spot where red blood is spreading on the side of my body,
There is still the provincial government building, the helicopters flying like dragonflies,
And the building that did not die under the high-altitude shooting.

On the spot where red blood is spreading on the side of my body,
There is naked pain, the sound of gunshots,
And the sturdy May sky,

* The "side" refers to the side of Jeonil Building, covered with bullet holes from a barrage of indiscriminate gunfire from military helicopters during the1980 Gwangju Uprising.

That even armored cars or tanks could not make a hole in.

Somehow, on the side of my body,
There are affectionate words,
On the tip of which sorrow is smeared;
The yukjabaegi tunes;
And either heat shimmers or tearful eyes;
And the mountain is moving into it.
To the place where the children of light are playing, **
The mountain has come down.
To the empty space on the side of my body.

** The "light" refers to the meaning of the syllable "gwang" in the name of the city "Gwangju."

POET'S NOTES

1

Up-down, left-right, front-back···. One ought to find "time" as the fourth dimension after them.

2

From old folktales, we learn that the world of life and the world of death are somehow connected. As civilization progresses, though, the world of death turns into something filthy and thus becomes expelled from the world of life. As a result, life and death are segregated into two completely different worlds. And they call this process "civilization."

Isn't this abyss between life and death too painful, though? That's why I imagine that, if we continue to walk, then we can reach the world of death, and again meet our loved ones there.

For example, I think of a space like the Peace Blossom Land in a fable written by Tao Yuan Ming (c. 365-427). It's not located somewhere we cannot reach, but a place we can get to through a very narrow way among rocky roads. And yet, that world beyond the narrow journey of rocky roads might clearly belong to a higher dimension than the one we know.

For example, we know from old tales that a goat can transform into a human being and relate with human beings in that higher-level world within a mountain valley. We know that a bear or tiger can also transform into a human being. These things can happen in the world of a higher dimension.

3

The bodies of organisms turn into soil, which then

becomes fuel, like peat. It heats our bodies, and then becomes smoke to pool in the sky. The time of soil, the life of humans, and the light of heaven are all connected with one another. And the spatial transforms into the temporal.

I call this "archeology"—because it excavates time from the space of underground.

4

Human language cannot express everything. We begin in the state of no language and afterward live in a society constructed by language. Then, after a long time, we realize that there are things that cannot be expressed in language. What Jacques Lacan called "the Real" is what a poet is trying to say. A poet tries to reach this place through language. But what we speak is always different from what we want to say. The distance between them is a world of endless desire. This is what humans are concerned with: the sea horizon and land horizon, and the sea between them. In other words, we cannot reach "the Real" that lies beyond language "through language." Perhaps this is that fate that poetry is struggling with?

I assume that there is a sort of entrance to "the Real." And this entrance is the goal for poems. What a poet wants to say is farther away, though, beyond that entrance. Poets die without reaching that faraway place. What we've lost is in that distant place. A poet sings that they will give us what we don't have. Or give us what they don't have. I say again: a poet cannot give us what we've lost. And nobody can give others what they don't have. A poet is simply circling around crazily in a wrong place—circling around something, around an object of "*jouissance.*" Some might consider this all in vain. But isn't love also doing something like that? To give what's not there, what we don't have, and what the poet doesn't have, what the poet cannot give?

5

"Lemon yellow" is a "thing." And we may call what's beyond it "eternity." We may call "eternity" by any name. Since whatever name we call is wrong, we may do so. However, if we define it so, it actually does not mean "eternal life." Of course, since eternal life is impossible, it's also close to what I want to talk about. However, to pursue eternal life in its dictionary meaning is also far from what I want to talk about. This negative way of describing is the only way I can talk about it.

6

I am lonely in the world created by God.

The phrase “festival of being” expresses the beauty of the world created by God. Originally, this is the name Mita Muneske gave to the world of literature by Miyazawa Kenji.*

The “festival of being” emphasizes the alienation of the subject watching it. To Miyazawa Kenji, nature was often harsh. He was an alienated being in it. I occasionally feel that, too; however, to me, being or phenomenon is not always harsh. As I see them, they see me, too. I dye them with my thoughts. In this process, my being transforms: I am beautiful, too. Through that sublimation, I can reconcile with God. This is what I want to express by the phrase “festival of being.”

* 見田宗介, 定本 見田宗介 著作集IX: 宮澤賢治—存在の祭りの中へ (岩波書店, 2012)

In order to depict a beautiful world, I combine four elements as Bachelard did: air, water, fire, and earth. In my poems *Lapland Post Office* (2013), *Lemon Yellow* (2018), and *Angukdong Shop for Crying 1.5* (2020), I focused on creating situations. I wrote poems like short stories. This time, I tried to sublate stories and create images. To do this, Bachelard was a good guide.

7

Confronting history in another way. The Jeju April 3 and the May Gwangju. Not to be obsessed by proper nouns. "Dark tourism" should not be retrieved as tourism. Dark tourism fixes people into a place, and later binds them with names. Many of my predecessors make history into the present by turning it into stories. It is moving. However, what has been happening afterward? Nowadays, everyone is turning history into stories. And they are repeated, and become mediocre things. Doing so is harming the brilliant achievements of my predecessors. Is dark tourism really mass producing the awakened? Historical sites are gradually becoming tourist attractions. Rather than being concerned about the names of places, we should pay attention to people's expressions and movements.

Incarnation. Events inscribed in nature. symbols sealed in a body. The Sewol Ferry. It's a matter of mourning. The boy is looking at the white moon in the underwater classroom. The skirt of the moonlight. Water mother.

8

To search for the truth, you enter the mountain

in search of a hermit. When you ask a boy under a pine tree about his whereabouts, he tells you that his master went to gather medicinal herbs. When you ask where the master would be, the boy says that, although his master would be in the mountains, he wouldn't know where, as the clouds are thick. A place where you cannot reach with language. A place that's impossible. A place that is blocked by the wall of clouds.

I am reminded of a poem by a Tang poet, Jia Dao. Although it has been more than 30 years since I read the poem, I still cannot forget it.

9

Chinkle-chankle is a word in the famous play by Peter Shaffer, *Equus*. Alan becomes a horse, holding chinkle-chankle in his mouth. It's a horse running freely. And it's interesting to become free while being muzzled. It enables you to gallop beyond language—because you cannot ordinarily speak while muzzled.

It has been already almost 20 years since I saw Shaffer's play. I must have seen it with either L majoring in Chinese literature or L majoring in English literature. The horses in that production were wearing costumes made from pieced-together leather and metal. I have heard that some recent performances feature horses wearing jeans. I'd like to see those performances, too.

10

This is my fifth book of poems. I feel that that I am writing poems seriously. For that, I am indebted to the late Seoung Chan-gyeong (1930-2013), who wrote poems more seriously than I. He was a disciple of beauty and also never stopped searching for the truth. I feel that I belong to a different world than his, that I stand in a much smaller world.

POET'S ESSAY

On the Road Downhill

I spent a few days in January in Okinawa. Misguided by the bone-chilling cold in Seoul, I brought a padded coat, but the weather in Okinawa was as balmy as spring time. On the day after my arrival, it poured heavy rain. Despite the rain, though, it wasn't cold.

Holding an umbrella, I went to Shurijo Castle: a wooden building in which gold and red live harmoniously together. It is a Chinese-style building. I toured the inside of it. Down a long corridor, a long line of tourists crawled, like a snake. Riding its back, I followed down the corridor. Afterward, I dropped by a tearoom and looked out at a garden in the rain, while drinking a specialty tea. The tea came with three cookies. Rather than the taste of the tea or the cookies, I enjoyed that moment of stillness. My most important memory of Shurijo Castle is that moment of stillness.

Outside of the castle was a narrow path taking one down to Kinjo Shitamachi. Somewhat hidden was a sign that read "The Most Beautiful Road in the World." I heard that it had originally been a much longer road, some kilometers long, and that it had been destroyed during World War II by bombing, and partially restored only in the 1980s.

This road is called "Ishidatamido." As the downhill path was slippery, I had to walk carefully, which made it quite a long trek to the end of the road. One crossroads intersected with a larger street for vehicles, which I passed. Altogether, I think I walked about a kilometer.

The entrance to the road was dark, shaded by a thick forest. Perhaps because of the rainy weather, it felt mysterious. A little down the road it was flanked by rows of houses on both sides. From that point on, I could look down at Kinjo Shitamachi in the distance, faraway. During this walk, I did not look back. As a result, the journey was inscribed in my mind going downhill. Even if I had looked back, I don't think I could have seen Shurijo Castle. As the castle is on top of a steep hill, I had gone up there only looking down at the road. So the Ishidatamido was indeed a road going downhill—it is a path you take after being relieved of all social responsibilities, where you become a natural human being. And a road of resignation. "The most beautiful road in the world" is a quiet path of resignation.

At the end of the road was a restaurant. On the surface of a small stone water mortar there, a couple of hibiscus petals floated. I drank cold beer and ate dried noodles. My glasses fogged up. As my transportation home was in the parking lot of the Shurijo Castle, I had to muster the energy and began walking up.

A Cat in the Bise Village

There is a village called Bise in a northern part of the main island of Okinawa. And there is a road there called Fukugi Road that is famous. I dropped by the village to look around.

At the entrance of the village, I found three cats resting. They did not move, even when I touched them. Also, a place was renting bicycles near the entrance. If I knew how to ride a bike, I probably would have rented one.

The "fukugi" in Fukugi Road is the name of a tree. It grows straight and its leaves are fairly thick. These trees were really thickly planted, and the entire village was surrounded by a road lined with these fukugi trees. It felt like I was in the middle of a maze.

Planting these trees so thickly was a way to block the wind. The sea breezes were fierce. I could not feel the wind on the road, but where the road ended and the beach was visible, gusty winds came off the sea. There was an old tree lying on the beach, which seemed to have been downed by the wind. A small boat was lying sideways there, with an unlikely vending machine next to it. The machine stood straight despite the gusty winds.

Fukugi Road was actually a bit boring. In the houses in Bise village, porcelain dolls were prominent. I first encountered a set of seven dolls from the Snow White and Seven Dwarfs story, but Snow White was missing. A sort of kitch, the kind of thing tourists might like. Also, on top of doors or walls of most houses were lion figures. Not just a single lion, but many of them. I wondered if Okinawans exchanged those dolls during their annual festivals. There were lions on the roofs as well.

Although the fukugi trees were a wind break, the forest also looked like it was hiding the village. When you reached the houses, after passing through this wall of fukugi, you encountered the lions keeping guard. So the houses were hidden behind two layers. These hidden houses looked strange but cozy.

On the Fukugi Road, I momentarily got lost and wandered around a bit. Then a bleary-eyed, tricolored cat that I'd seen at the entrance approached me, rubbed its body on the back of my foot, and left. I followed it to the entrance of the village. A brief encounter.

As the eateries in the village were all fully occupied, I went to another place to have lunch. I cannot remember much about it, but I think I might have eaten a pork cutlet. I cannot remember its taste, but it was delicious. It came with a side dish of tofu with a tiny fish on top. Or It might have been a dish in its own right. At any rate, I cannot remember where this restaurant was located.

A poet went on a journey to search for his dead sister. He took a train. The train ran to Karafuto rather than Sakhalin. It was a journey inside an apple. This is Miyazawa Kenji's story. There is a scene featuring a passing train in the "xxx" chapter of his *Night of the Milky Way Railroad* (1934):

He could hear the sound of train. The windows of small trains looked small and red. Imagining many travelers in it, peeling apples and laughing, Giovanni fell into an unspeakable sadness and again looked up at the sky.

Giovanni is an object of ridicule among his classmates. For some reason, his peers are ostracizing him. Unable to play with them, he goes up a hill where there is a wheel-like structure. Up there he can see beautiful lights from the village. A train passes by. The light inside its windows look warm and inviting. It contrasts with the world of gloom and darkness where he lives. It makes him even sadder. Giovanni feels alienated. It's a scene that anybody can understand.

And in this scene there appears an apple. It is a symbol, but one that cannot be replaced by an egg or something else. This apple that has a symbolic meaning appears six or seven times in *Night of the Milky Way Railroad*. And that's not all: It appears again in his poem "Aomori Elegy" (1923). As the first drafts of this novel and poem were written around the same time, this repetition may not be especially odd:

On a field in a pitch-black night like this,

The windows of train cars become glass panes in an aquarium.

(Just like the procession of utility poles
Hurriedly changing places,
The train runs into the brilliant lens of the Milky Way,
A giant hydrogen apple)
It runs inside an apple.

After the death of his sister Toshiko, Miyazawa Kenji travels through Aomori and Hokkaido, crosses the Soya Strait, and reaches Karafuto—currently called Sakhalin. His apparent reason is to do a research about jobs for his students, but behind it lies another mission: finding the whereabouts of his dead sister.

The first seven lines of "Aomori Elegy" (1923) became an important motif in *Night of the Milky Way Railroad.* In it, the peculiar idea of a train running inside an apple is presented. Here the apple symbolizes the universe. Also, the same metaphor of a train "inside an apple" is found, for example, in the following passage in *Night of the Milky Way Railroad*: "And in a moment, the cross was in front of the window, and I could see a ring-shaped, bluish cloud, like the flesh of an apple, slowly, slowly circling around."

The first two lines of the above poem correspond to the night train scene in which Giovanni watches it on top of the hill of "the column of a wheel." The only difference is whether you see it from inside or outside the train. From inside, the observer receives the speed of a new modern civilization's product through their physical sense organs. Giovanni says, "I am a wonderful engine locomotive. As I am on a slope, I'm fast."

But why on earth an "apple"? It is a symbol that that must be clarified to understand Miyazawa Kenji's universe. In "Giovanni's Ticket," the last chapter of *Night of the Milky Way Railroad*, an apple is frequently mentioned. Campanella suddenly says, "Somehow I can smell the fragrance of an apple.

Is it because I think of an apple now?" In fact, it is a world where whatever you imagine is certain to come true. This question of Campanella's is answered in a later scene, in which a character who is presumably a lighthouse-keeper hands him an apple, saying, "How about this? You've never seen an apple like this, right?" The fragrance of an apple could have been from this one that the lighthouse-keeper had. But is that it?

Campanella's question is raised immediately before a young man and a young brother and sister appear from nowhere, while a bird-catcher suddenly disappears. The threesome are suddenly found on a train, when the ship they were on board collides with an iceberg and is wrecked. They call it "God's invitation." This phenomenon could be a sort of spatial distortion, a dimensional contortion. And this has something to do with an apple:

"Oh, I just saw my mom in my dream. At a place where there was a handsome bookcase and books, mom gave me her hand and smiled gently. I woke up at the moment I said, 'Shall I bring you an apple?' Oh, this is inside that train before, isn't it?"

"Here it is, the apple from your dream. This gentleman gave it to you."

The apple in a dream is connected to one in reality, although this reality is a sort of a dream, too. The apple connects the dream and reality, as well as inside and outside. It also expresses the structure of the Milky Way.

An apple is not a simple sphere, of course but one with a depression. In other words, there is an area where the surface skin is being sucked inside of it. It will also reach an ovary. The outside is transformed into the inside. Like the structure of a Klein bottle. To Miyazawa Kenji, the Milky Way is a world in a higher dimension than the world of three dimensions, where inside and outside are indistinguishable, like an apple. For a detailed discussion of this, I recommend that a book about Miyazawa Kenji by Mita Muneske. *

Fish Cake House

In the evening of the last day of my Okinawa trip, I went to a fish cake house near my lodgings. I could not go to any better one, since there were too many customers in them. So I went to the most shabby-looking one—sort of a pub, where an elderly lady was taking care of everything. The aroma of the fish cake was impressive, though. When I said that the place looked historical, she responded with a short, "Does it?" perhaps considering my

* See also the "Poet's Note" in this book.

remark as a sort of put-down about its appearance. When I again said the place looked like it had a long tradition, she said that it had been around for about 30 years. In it there were many steel containers with thick broth in them, from which you serve what you wanted; the woman scooped from them to fill bowls. When I said I wanted to eat a fish cake, she said, pointing to all containers, that they were all fish cakes, including ones with eggs, devil's tongue jelly, and turnips. I ordered many different things, wanting to try them all. They indeed tasted wonderful.

The woman was entirely absorbed in watching TV. I tried to chat with her a bit, and watch TV with her, but we could not communicate very well across the language barrier between us.

Osaka, In Search of a Hotel

I walked a lot in Osaka. I liked it. Although I made many trial-and-error mistakes, now I would like to return to those mistakes. No one scolded me for making mistakes, rather, everyone seemed to care about me, someone fumbling around like a fool.

It was my first time visiting Osaka. I boarded a plane at 5:10 pm in Jeju and flew for about an hour. I had made a reservation at a small hotel near Nihonbashi. From the airport, I transferred to the Nankai Electric Railway.

The train has an enormous roar. After about 40 minutes, I got off at Namba Station, which was crowded. And there were so many shopping malls around it that I felt utterly confused. As Nihonbashi was supposed to be only one station away, I decided to get out of the station and stroll toward my hotel. It was foolish of me to think I could do that. To begin with, I could not find an exit from the station, so I wandered around inside for a while, and ended up buying a few postcards at a gift shop. I also found and dropped in a bookstore and looked around. In fact, if I had used the map that a student had lent me, I could have easily found transfer information, but I was in too much of a daze.

After exiting the station, without much thought I began walking in the direction that seemed to lead me to Nihonbashi. After a while, I found myself in the Ebisucho neighborhood. By then, I had walked quite a distance, an hour or so, and my legs hurt. Fortunately, I could reach Ebisucho Station of the Osaka Metro Sakaisuji Line. I thought that I could easily find my hotel once I arrived at the Nihonbashi Station, as I had the address. I should have taken taxi.

When I got off at Nihonbashi Station, I again began wandering, relying on the address. I again ended up walking some 30 or 40 minutes. Exhausted, I encountered a police officer, whom I asked for directions. He checked a map application on his phone and told me where to go. It turned out that I had been wandering in a completely wrong area.

It's not like I didn't have a map application either—I wasn't completely hopeless about modern technology. But I couldn't get internet service. I had bought portable Wi-Fi in the airport before leaving Korea, but it didn't work. To speak honestly, though, I am actually someone who is hopeless about modern technology.

The hotel room was smaller than I had expected. I thought of washing before sleeping, but was worried that I might catch a cold. Instead, I drank a cup of tea, preparing it in the room. It was tasty; but then they switched the brand from the next day, and I didn't find it very tasty. Although I walked a lot, and was exhausted, I could not fall asleep for a long time that night.

A Used Bookstore

I had breakfast early in the morning at the hotel restaurant. My most important goal that day was to drop by a used bookstore near Ebisucho Station of the Osaka Metro Sakaisuji Line. It was a store I happened to find on an internet search a day before my departure to Osaka. On the internet, though, there was no address, but only a rough map. And I made the same mistake as the day before: I imagined I could easily find it as long as I went to the area near the station.

I thought I had wandered around the Ebisucho Station long enough the evening before to know it. But the daytime looked entirely different. What unfolded before me was a street of *otakus*. As it was rather early in the morning, the shops were all closed. The bookstore for which I was looking was supposed to be open from 1 to 5 in the winter. So I wandered around the neighborhood, and it began to rain.

I decided to drop by a tourist information center. A single older gentleman there was wearing an orange jumper. When I asked him if he knew the location of the used bookstore "K" he made some phone calls. Then he handed me a Korean-language Ebisucho map in which he marked the location.

During lunch, restaurants were all crowded. As I was not used to eating in such places alone, I looked around for a less crowded restaurant. I walked around where I had wandered before. There was many guesthouses in the neighborhood and small hotels. I entered a café attached to a hostel and ordered a beef lunch. At first, a few older men were eating at a table, but afterward a young man in a suit, perhaps a professional worker from nearby, and a Chinese family entered. The young man looked to be in his mid-20s. Carrying an umbrella, he ate at a table near the window and watched the rain. He looked graceful, as he ate very slowly. The Chinese family sat around two tables put together. It took them long time to order. The family included both elderly members and children. I was leaving by the time they ordered dessert.

With the map I had been given at the information, I began searching for the used bookstore called K. The bookstore I found was called Shibutani Bookstore. It was still closed, perhaps preparing to open. I wandered the area for another hour or so before going back to it. The store was a tiny space. As I didn't want to bring in my wet umbrella, I gestured to leave it outside, but they told me to bring it inside. But they did not have the books I was looking for. When I showed them the list, they said they did not have them in stock at the time. *Are "K"and*

Shibutani the same place? I labored in vain today. Thinking like that, I felt a bit depressed. But then the owner, noticing the name "K" in my notebook, said I wasn't at the right place, and he would take me there. It turned out that "K" was tucked in a corner of a building a block away. It was difficult to find, if you were visiting for the first time—it did not even have a sign. Without the help of the owner of the Shibutani Bookstore I could not have found it.

But the books I was looking for were not there either. Still, I could buy *Osaka* (1939) by Ono Tozaburo. Then, after doing some shopping in the Namba City mall, I returned to the hotel in the evening. After watching a TV show in which the magician Daigo and sociologist Furuichi Noritoshi engaged in some psychological confrontation, I went to bed. After a shallow sleep, I woke and tossed for a long time.

Kim Hui-gu was an amateur poet, a member of the coterie magazine *Azaleas* (1953-58), led by Kim Si-jong. Established under the command of the Japanese Communist Party, *Azaleas* was controlled by the Pro-Pyeongyang Federation of Korean Residents in Japan. The federation tried to use the magazine to propagandize for an idealized image of North Korea. Its members, though, including Kim Si-jong, thought that talking about the lives of Korean residents in Japan was more important than idealizing North Korea.

Azaleas was a comfort that Korean residents desperately needed to survive in Japanese society, with its severe discrimination. As a result, Kim Si-jong's relationship with the Pro-Pyongyang Federation of Korean Residents in Japan became conflicted.

Ono Tozaburo, a man in high esteem in Osaka,

helped *Azaleas* from the sidelines. A postcard from him, praising a poem by Kim Hui-gu, was published in the 5th issue of the magazine. In the poem, Kim Hui-gu uses Tsuruhashi Station as a symbolic witness of Koreans living in Japan. This station was an intimate eyewitness to the difficult lives and sorrows of these first-generation Koreans in Japan. It was a place where they were living with dirt. Kim Hui-gu focused on the depiction of places representing Koreans in Japan in his poems "Street Corners in Osaka" (*Azaleas* #5) and "Ikaino" (*Azaleas* #6). But his dauntless courage was eventually crushed by Japanese society's discrimination against Koreans and the postwar poverty he could not avoid. After publishing "Prayer" (*Azaleas* #11), Kim Hui-gu disappeared. He had thrown himself under a train. The poems Cho Sam-ryong's "Morning of a Suicide" and Kang Cheong-ja's "At a Corner in Osaka," in *Azaleas* #14, seem to be their responses to his suicide. In his poem Cho Sam-ryong wrote: "From the inner pocket/He took out a foreigner registration card and a work card./Work days 10./Three days ago/ In a weak voice/He said, "I don't have work today, again."/Could he no longer bear it?" Words like "foreigner registration card" and "work card" intimately convey the reality of Koreans in Japan at that time.

By throwing himself under a train of the Osaka Loop Line, Kim Hui-gu's body was destroyed, but his spirit is still hovering around cold downtown Osaka along the line.

Homeland

Living in Osaka are many Korean immigrants, who originally came from Jeju Island. Among these immigrants who went to Japan during the Jeju April 3 Incident is Kim Si-jong. Further, many Koreans living in Japan have insisted on maintaining their nationality as that of an undivided Korea. It deserves to be called by that label: "the belief of the nationality of an undivided Korea." Although the word they use for Korea is "Joseon," from the Joseon dynasty, it does not signify just North Korea, which still uses this moniker, although some people mistakenly think that. It simply means that they consider their homeland to be Korea before its division. Most Korean residents in Japan came there during the time of Japanese imperialist occupation of Korea in 1910-45. In other words, when they went to Japan, they were Koreans under colonial rule. Although the Japanese argued that "Japan and Korea are One" during World War II, after their defeat, they marginalized Koreans in Japan as foreigners.

Overnight, Koreans in Japan found themselves without a nationality who had to register as foreigners. The procedure was not simple either. Their homeland was devastated during World War II and then divided. So they lost a homeland. I cannot help becoming solemn about this, considering that they insisted on their nationality of one Korea, even while they gave up many benefits by acquiring South Korean citizenship, including the freedom of visiting their hometowns.

In a symposium about the Jeju April 3 Incident, the question was raised whether or not the incident is a part of South Korean history. Some Koreans living in the Kansai region remonstrated, asking where they would belong, if this incident is included in South Korean history. Others wondered, with a sigh, which "history" their Japanese spouses belonged to. So it was a tragedy that went beyond the boundary of a country.

This argument that the tragedy of Koreans in Japan, who originally came from Jeju Island, exists across national boundaries is thought-provoking.

But I feel it necessary to think of the Republic of Korea as a dream, different from the result of existing historical processes. Although there were many different groups among those involved in the Jeju April 3 Incident, I feel that we need to acknowledge the dream of the people who opposed the separate election in the South in 1948. Even if that dream might have returned to us as disillusionment, we, as their descendants, should not treat their vision as meaningless. When we think of the history of the Republic of Korea, we don't have to insist on the history as it happened, the one we learned as students—it does not always coincide with people's memories. Might we not think of today's Republic of Korea as having been created as a result of the dreams experienced by the victims of the Jeju April 3 Incident or the May 18 Uprising? In this light, I consider Koreans in Japan who insist on Korean nationality before division, including Koreans who escaped to Japan during the Jeju April 3 Incident, as a part of the history of the Republic of Korea. In this light, wouldn't it be a legitimate task to trace their footsteps in the history of Korean literature aspiring for Korean unification?

The End of an Era

I thought of visiting Kyoto for a day, but decided not to. I had breakfast at the same place as the morning before. Then I took the Sennichimae Line to Tsuruhashi and Imazato, where it is known that many Koreans in Japan reside. In Tsuruhashi, many restaurants offered *bulgogi* and *naengmyeon*. Along the main road were quite a few medical clinics. As I became curious about novels by Furuichi Noritoshi, after watching a TV program talking about his works, I dropped by a bookstore in the area and looked for them. Although I remembered seeing them displayed in a large bookstore at the Namba City Mall, I couldn't find any copies in that neighborhood bookstore.

I did a stupid thing that day: I left my room without my key. And the lock was the kind that locked on its own. Realizing it belatedly, I returned to the hotel and explained the situation to the front desk, who told me that I had to pay 500 yen. It seemed that he misunderstood me and thought that I lost the key rather than leaving it in the room. And the language barrier was too great for me to correct his misunderstanding.

I finally bought novels by Furuichi Noritoshi at the Namba City. He is also a sociologist, and one of his books, *The Happy Youth of a Desperate Country*, was translated into Korean and published in 2014. For a sociology book, I believe it was sold well in Korea. However, as a sociologist, he was in an ambiguous position—that is, he is not a typical academic. He was also a kind of entertainer featured often on TV. His novel *Goodbye, Mr. Hitonari* was attracting attention, also because of his personality. His novel was displaying prominently on a stand in that big bookstore. *Goodbye, Mr. Hitonari* also might have been spotlighted because the Japanese were facing the end of the Heisei era, because Chinese characters of the name "Hitonari" can also be pronounced "Heisei." The protagonist's social position was similar to that of the author: someone with alove affair typical of the Heisei era. Not surprisingly perhaps, it read like a sort of sociological history rather than a novel, featuring men who do not like sex, the issues of euthanasia and artificial intelligence, epicurism among young people in Tokyo, and their dating routines, fashion, and living arrangements.

As I still had some time after looking around the bookstore, I watched a movie in the Namba Park

Cinema, *Twelve Children Who Want to Die*. There were only about 20 people in the theater, as it was in the early afternoon. I expected it to be a good mystery, but it did not have an elaborate plot. A girl in the movie was wearing "Goth look" clothes, which made her look like a doll. Pathetically, adult men at a back row made loud comments over and over, about how cute she was.

Slapstick

I went to Kansai Airport, after transferring to the Nankai Line at Namba Station. Many people heading toward the airport were carrying large pieces of luggage. Some were Koreans rushing to return and others Japanese tourists. I seemed to be the only person without luggage.

The train again moved with a roar. Looking outside, I realized that we were on a railway bridge stretching over the sea; I hadn't noticed it when I arrived at night.

In the airport, I was at a loss again: I thought I had to take a monorail to the terminal, but I could not find it. As there was only a shuttle, I took it to Terminal 2; however, when I arrived, I realized it was a terminal exclusively for J Airline. I rushed to take the shuttle again back to Terminal 1, and barely make it to check-in.

I arrived at the Jeju Airport in two hours. Freed from the constant stress of a foreign language, I was relieved. After returning the portable WIFI, I returned home. Will my next trip be a bit better?

At home, I threw all the clothes I had worn into the washing machine. As I had worn many layers, they were all sweaty, even in the middle of winter. While listening to the whirring sound of the washing machine, I called mother, to let her know I was back safely.

In Osaka, I wandered the streets, and did not feel pressured by time. Except for the poetry book by Ono Tozaburo, all the books I had bought in Japan have been translated into Korean since then. I feel like I wasted some time and effort, but it does not bother me much. The movie I saw in Japan was also shown in Korea afterward. I could probably understand it better with subtitles. But I won't watch it again.

COMMENTARY

Poems Placed Beside Death

Kim Sang-hyeok

In this essay, I'd like to talk about why this book's first poem, "Midday," should be read twice. In some of his poems, including this one, Jang I-ji depicts various aspects of utopia. This utopia is understood to be a sort of impossibility, where the poetic object *you*, another ideal, is absent ("Rosy Cheeks, White Hair"). It is presented as an illusion, projected onto the work of a painter ("Waterfall"), and causes the poetic speaker only sadness, as it is represented as something broken within reality ("Early Summer"). It is a world that reveals itself as a voice without a face

("Hibiscus"), a space that can be perceived only momentarily, through the innocence of a child ("Search for the Sky"), and thus it is the sound of bygone laughter ("On a Autumn Night") or the sky not found in this world ("The Most Beautiful Five Minutes in This World").

As the idea of utopia is oriented toward "not now" or "not here," lyrical poems by classicists, including Jang I-ji, cannot help being alert to simple sentimentalism. The place where utopia exists is not here, and the time it comes true cannot be now. Thus, a book of poems depicting utopian space and time might inevitably adopt elements such as exotic places and people, reconstructed history or childhood, or a defense of and referral to classical arts. Nevertheless, the tag of sentimentalism would be an index: criticizing sentences and images that are not so new in a work, rather than a global criticism aimed at the general sensibility of an authors' works. For example, the lyrical depiction of a family's labor and their dinner table in Jang's poem "Scotland" is even more fantastically vivid and strangely moving—exactly because it uses a "foreign" country as its backdrop.

Other poems in this book also have as clear a poetic strategy as "Scotland." "Waterfall" has the name of a painter well known for his "Waterfall" series, Senju Hiroshi, as its subtitle. This poem compares the moment when stars pour down onto the scene, where the sky and earth can't be distinguished, with a waterfall. And, yet, a strange and fantastical atmosphere is added to this poem, seemingly insisting on classical lyricism, exactly because of its title and subtitle, both of which function strategically to add such a specific effect.

It is for the same effect that the poet intentionally inserts foreign terms and Chinese characters throughout his poems, such as "Shape Shift," in the subtitle of the poem "Searching for the Sky," "Roland

Barthes," the subtitle of the poem "Blue Ink," the quotation between the title and poem in "Chinkle-Chankle," or the footnote "emperor angelfish," for its Korean name in "Although We Might Live While Forgetting All About Our Childhood."

Together with what I've discussed so far, it might also be worth noting that the poet constructs a utopian space particularly along the temporal axis of the past, and that he tends to scrutinize the images of sky and water. For example, let's look at "Water Mother," a result of his love for the past and for the image of water. At the moment when a boy visiting an aquarium with his mother shakes his mother's skirt and the mother holds his hand, when this moment overlaps with the image of jellyfish floating inside the aquarium, the "water mother," a nickname for jellyfish, acquires the imagery of copious and transparent love. For another superb image, we may look at "Searching for the Sky." Beginning with a familiar association between the color of the sky and the sea, the poem depicts a naïve child's gathering of shells, while squatting on the beach, and thinking "the real sky is inside the pink butterfly shell." Through this image, a highly abstract act of "searching for the sky" is represented in the fingertips of a child rummaging through a shell mound.

*

Considering the achievements of the poems I have described partially above, it is ironic that the texture of "Midday" is quite prominently heterogeneous among them. As the first poem opening the book, it plays the role of a signpost, guiding the reader into the space of the poet's innermost thoughts. As a signpost, it is a boundary that divides the sensibility inside this book from the outside experience of the reader. At the same time, "Midday" is a bow protruding above or outside the reality of the poem. As a signpost, it performs its function as a guide, above all, through its intuitive form. Also, it is the most secondary poem, in that it does not have any context without the space unfolding behind it, while at the same time it has a unique value in this book, in that it greets visitors/readers before any other place/poem.

The irony in “Midday” as a signpost is that the emotion it conveys is extremely ordinary and good-hearted. Beginning with “There are people living in villages both before and behind!/How wonderful it is to be able to see other people!,” the poem calls neighbors “other people,” rather than “neighbors,” but at the same time describes how the speaker is able to see them as the most joyful thing in the world. In this poem, we find neither exotic emotions nor the time of the past, which temporarily represent utopia, nor a confusion with other artistic forms. It does not seem like it should be easy to fascinate readers with the kind of simple and ordinary utterance in it: "it is great··· to watch dandelion spores flying and fluttering," or the depiction of spores flying and fluttering as "that weightless clouds' practice" to fascinate readers. This space of midday, described like a utopia, only includes a simple sentimentalism, indeed, one that seems to regress into a pastoral scenery that is quite unrelated to our contemporary life.

To go to my conclusion, this simple sensibility in "Midday" transforms into a tragic emotion *after* a reader has read the entire book. This occurs because of a few poems that do not fit easily into the atmosphere of this collection. "Then All The Light" deals with the Jeju April 3 Incident, an object of deep interest to this poet for a long time. The space depicted in "An Ark" above all is the May Gwangju, the name of the city that rhymes with "*bangju*," the

Korean word for "ark," but it is also a deck where all the souls killed in many different places gather and have conversations among themselves. The first stanza of "Song of a Side" presents the image of the indiscriminate shooting that a helicopter poured onto the side of the Jeonil Building during the Gwangju Uprising.

Although only a few poems deal with tragedies in modern Korean history in this book, their placement close together in the latter part leaves a deep impression on readers. When the reader closes the book, the images whirling around in their minds are not those of vivid, exotic flavors nor an aesthetically romanticized past. In fact, readers will think of all the beautiful scenes they encountered in the first half of the book in relation to the lives lost under the wheels of violent history. For example, although the depression in an apple is compared with dimples on the smiling face of a child, an apple next to a damaged body cannot help reminding us of the penetration and holes many bullets and slashes.

What Jang's poetic language sharply reveals is that the most precious treasure that the dead are deprived of is none other than ordinary life. In "Then All The Light," people who escape punitive forces to the mountain are repeatedly reminded of their homes, the space for their ordinary lives. While reading "An Ark" readers will pay full attention and with full emotions to the scene, where "boys who look like high school students are taking water-green selfies against the backdrop of the forest of Seongpanak Peak." While reading the poem, we instinctively realize how precious to the dead must be the everyday joy those high school students enjoy. No one will be ignorant of the fact that "affectionate words" and "*yukjabaegi* tunes" mentioned in "Song of a Side" are the products of uneventful everyday lives.

At this point, return to the extremely ordinary scene in "Midday," in which people are living in villages both before and behind—and look at it carefully. The life in which one sees people alive, the ordinary life in which one can greet those living people, is not at all ordinary.

*

Although I can't recall his exact words, in an interview with a literary magazine in 2015, I remember Mr. Jang I-ji saying that his life as a poet was over. It might have been the casual rhetoric of an artist who had composed good poems for a long time, or it could have been an expression of his cynicism at that moment. It could be, though, that he thought he had passed his prime. However, on finishing my reading his fifth book, I felt that I could enjoy many more books like this one. I haven't yet encountered poems placed beside death without hesitation this much and this frighteningly.

WHAT THEY SAY ABOUT JANG I-JI

Jang I-ji's poems try to verify the world through stories that continue indefinitely. The phrase "finally at a point where a story is about to begin" in his poem "Sherbet Land, Writing Degree Zero," in *Angukdong Shop for Crying*, comes to mind. In his new book of poems, *Lemon Yellow*, he continues to tell stories yet-to-be completed, as in "Coffee Pot" and "Laughing Villain," giving us a sense of his belief in the world not entirely revealed—like other people's thoughts. Incidents that "are still remembered, although they happened more than a decade ago ("Coffee Pot")," "the smile of that day still occasionally coming to mind ("Laughing Villain")" for no reason, or the mind of a mother who made a snowman with her two sons on the rooftop one day instead of going out to sell things as usual ("Southern Sky")—all are fragments of a mysteriously opaque world, no matter how much one thinks about it, with scenes whose meaning cannot be clearly explained, yet they are also "the Real," which shines with a brighter and more beautiful light than any memory.

Jang Eun-young (literary critic)

Crossing time and space—from childhood to youth, from the world of the web to a redevelopment area—and even crossing the time and space of super-time and no-place, we've examined Mr. J's "life unknown to others" in Jang I-ji's poem "Nonsense." Thus, we can read *Lapland Post Office* as a gloomy letter, with J as its message. Nonetheless, we should remember above all the solid contemporariness of Mr. J's old sadness and gloominess. His contemporariness also applies to the sensitive and direct look at the nuclear capitalism in his "Flat" and "Machines" series, as well as his poetic exploration of poverty and labor in postmodern times. In a tragic world, individuals suffer from depression. While overlaying his own concrete, everyday life with the phenomena of poverty in our times, as an integral part, Jang I-ji poignantly represents the lives of the "gloomy refugees" of our times.

Kim Young-hee (literary critic)

K-Poet
A Boy Is Looking at the White Moon from a Classroom Under the Sea

Written by Jang I-ji | **Translated by** Jeon Seung-hee
Published by ASIA Publishers | 445, Hoedong-gil, Paju-si, Gyeonggi-do, Korea
(Seoul Office: 161-1, Seodal-ro, Dongjak-gu, Seoul, Korea)
Homepage Address www.bookasia.org | **Tel** (822).821.5055 | **Fax** (822).821.5057
ISBN 979-11-5662-317-5 (set) | 979-11-5662-525-4 (04810)
First published in Korea by ASIA Publishers 2020

This book is published with the support of the Literature Translation Institute of Korea (LTI Korea).